P9-BJU-549

THE BAR MITZVAH BOOK

HUGH LAUTER LEVIN ASSOCIATES, INC.

ILLUSTRATIONS

TORAH ARK
19th century
wood, carved, gilt and painted
Poland
6½ × 42½"
Hebrew Union College Skirball Museum, Los Angeles
Photograph: John Reed Forsman

Emanuel de Witte
PORTUGUESE SYNAGOGUE IN AMSTERDAM
1680
oil on canvas
43¼ × 39"
Rijksmuseum, Amsterdam

Moritz Oppenheim
THE BAR MITZVAH SPEECH
Oscar Gruss Collection
Photograph: Thomas Feist

Edouard Brandon
BAR MITZVAH
oil on canvas
15 × 24¼"
The Israel Museum, Jerusalem

WIMPEL OF GERSHON, SON OF ABRAHAM SELTZ (detail)
1834
undyed linen, polychrome pigments
Germany
132 × 6½"
Hebrew Union College Skirball Museum, Los Angeles
Photograph: Erich J. Hockley

Moritz Oppenheim
THE RABBI'S BLESSING
Oscar Gruss Collection
Photograph: Thomas Feist

KIDDUSH CUP
18th century
silver
Danzig
6"
Moriah Antique Judaica, New York
Photograph: Thomas Feist

Jeremiah Zobel
RIMMONIM (Torah Finials)
Early 18th century
silver, parcel gilt
Frankfurt am Main
Hebrew Union College Skirball Museum, Los Angeles
Photograph: Erich J. Hockley

TORAH CURTAIN (center section)
1795
brocaded silk on linen
Galizia
60 × 36" (full size)
Moriah Antique Judaica, New York
Photograph: Thomas Feist

TALLIT, TALLIT BAG, AND TEFILLIN BAG
1904
silk with silk embroidery
China
84 × 29½", 11 × 8½", 5½ × 5½"
Hebrew Union College Skirball Museum, Los Angeles
Gift of Mr. and Mrs. Revan Komaroff
Photograph: John Reed Forsman

READER'S DESK
c. 1900
painted wood
Persia
16 × 22 × 18"
Moriah Antique Judaica, New York
Photograph: Thomas Feist

Rembrandt van Rijn
MOSES LIFTING THE TABLETS OF THE LAW
1659
oil on canvas
65¾ × 53"
Gemaldegalerie, Berlin-Dahlen

BAR MITZVAH COAT
19th century
Bucharan
The Israel Museum, Jerusalem

Isidor Kaufman
STUDYING THE TALMUD
Oscar Gruss Collection
Photograph: Thomas Feist

TORAH CASE
17th century
wood, gilt, red lacquer, and bronze
Kaifeng, China
30"
Hebrew Union College Skirball Museum, Los Angeles
Photograph: John Reed Forsman

Picture research: Ann Levy

Calligraphy: Jeanne Greco

Copyright © 1987 Hugh Lauter Levin Associates, Inc.
Printed in China
ISBN 0-88363-482-1

CONTENTS

TORAH ARK—Poland, 19th century

My son, strive to know yourself, to know and understand your Judaism, your wonderful, unique history, the inseparable connection of your people with the patriarchs and the prophets. You will then realize that you are part of the religious-national covenant of Israel, of the Holy Ark, an exemplar of the very covering of the Ark! You will be proud of your historic people and happy in your sublime faith.

From a message by
Dr. Isaac Halevi Herzog
Chief Rabbi of Israel

REJOICE, O YOUNG MAN, IN THY YOUTH.

Ecclesiastes 11:9

MY ENGLISH NAME

_____

MY HEBREW NAME

_____

THE DATE OF MY BIRTH

_____

THE HEBREW DATE OF MY BIRTH.

_____

THE PLACE I WAS BORN

_____

THE DATE OF MY BAR MITZVAH SERVICE

_____

THE HEBREW DATE OF MY BAR MITZVAH
SERVICE _____

PASTE PICTURE HERE

THE BEGINNING OF WISDOM IS: GET WISDOM;
YEA, WITH ALL THY GETTING GET UNDERSTANDING.

PROVERBS 4:7

THE NAME OF THE SYNAGOGUE

_____

THE ADDRESS OF THE SYNAGOGUE

_____

_____

THE SYNAGOGUE WAS FOUNDED ON

_____

THE NAME OF THE RABBI

_____

THE NAME OF THE CANTOR

_____

MY TEACHER'S NAME

_____

8

© 1997 Hugh Lauter Levin Associates, Inc.

PORTUGUESE SYNAGOGUE IN AMSTERDAM—Emanuel de Witte

A WISE SON MAKETH A GLAD FATHER...

PROVERBS 10:1

My Father

MY FATHER'S NAME

MY FATHER'S HEBREW NAME

The date of his birth

The place of his birth

My father's mother

Her hebrew name

The date of her birth

The place of her birth

My father's father

His hebrew name

The date of his birth

The place of his birth

As a joyful mother of children.
hallelujah

Psalm 113:9

My Mother

_____
MY MOTHER'S NAME

_____
MY MOTHER'S HEBREW NAME

_____
THE DATE OF HER BIRTH

_____
THE PLACE OF HER BIRTH

_____	_____
MY MOTHER'S MOTHER	MY MOTHER'S FATHER
_____	_____
HER HEBREW NAME	HIS HEBREW NAME
_____	_____
THE DATE OF HER BIRTH	THE DATE OF HIS BIRTH
_____	_____
THE PLACE OF HER BIRTH	THE PLACE OF HIS BIRTH

11

Other Members Of My Family

Write the English and Hebrew names, dates of birth, and other information about your brother(s), sister(s), and any other close relatives below.

_____   _____

_____   _____

_____   _____

_____   _____

_____   _____

_____   _____

_____   _____

_____   _____

_____   _____

_____   _____

THE BAR MITZVAH SPEECH—Moritz Oppenheim

My Hebrew school

_____

The address of the school

_____

My teachers

_____

When I first attended the school

_____

When I first learned Hebrew

_____

When I first began to study my haftarah _____

My tallit came from

_____

My tefillin came from

_____

My kippah came from

_____

Thine is the dew of thy youth.

Psalm 110:3

What I wore

_____

What my mother wore

_____

What my father wore

_____

What my brother(s) wore

_____

What my sister(s) wore

_____

Special parties held in my honor
before the day of the ceremony

_____

_____

The weather on the day of the
ceremony _____

_____

LET THE WORDS OF MY MOUTH AND THE
MEDITATION OF MY HEART BE ACCEPTABLE
BEFORE THEE, O LORD, MY ROCK, AND
MY REDEEMER.

Psalm 19:15

The Readings

Torah Portion _____

_____

_____

_____

Haftarah _____

_____

_____

_____

Special Prayers _____

_____

_____

_____

BAR MITZVAH—Edouard Brandon

Blessed is the man that trusteth in
the lord, and whose trust the lord is.

Jeremiah 17:7

Aliyot

First Aliyah-Rishon _____

Second Aliyah-Sheni _____

Third Aliyah-Shlishi _____

Fourth Aliyah-Revi'i _____

Fifth Aliyah-Hamishi _____

Sixth Aliyah-Shishi _____

Seventh Aliyah-Shvi'i _____

Hamagbiah (Torah Holder)

_____

Hagolel (Torah Dresser)

_____

This is my special prayer on the day of my Bar Mitzvah

_____

_____

_____

_____

_____

_____

_____

_____

_____

_____

_____

_____

WHAT I FELT WHEN I ENTERED THE SYNAGOGUE _____

_____

WHAT I FELT BEFORE THE CEREMONY

_____

_____

WHAT I FELT DURING THE CEREMONY

_____

_____

HOW MY READING WENT

_____

_____

WHAT I FELT AFTER THE CEREMONY

_____

_____

WIMPEL OF GERSHON, SON OF ABRAHAM SELTZ (detail)—Germany, 1834

he whom thou blessest is blessed.

NUMBERS 22:6

_____

_____

_____

_____

_____

_____

_____

_____

_____

_____

_____

_____

_____

TRAIN UP A CHILD IN THE WAY HE SHOULD
GO, AND EVEN WHEN HE IS OLD, HE WILL NOT
DEPART FROM IT.   PROVERBS 22:6

_____

_____

_____

_____

_____

_____

_____

_____

_____

_____

_____

_____

_____

_____

_____

_____

_____

_____

_____

_____

_____

_____

_____

_____

_____

_____

_____

_____

_____
SIGNATURE

THE RABBI'S BLESSING—Moritz Oppenheim

he hath consecrated his guests.

Zephaniah 1:7

Special events

_____

_____

_____

Special guests

_____

_____

_____

Special out-of-town visitors

_____

_____

_____

_____

AND he made them a feast,
AND they did eat AND drink.

GENESIS 26:30

PASTE
INVITATION HERE

But he that is of merry heart
hath a continual feast.

PROVERBS 15:15

When the party was held

_____

Where the party was held

_____

Special decorations

_____

Special entertainment

_____

Music _____

_____

Other _____

_____

שלשה כתרים

כתר תורה

KIDDUSH CUP—Danzig, 18th century

A feast is made for laughter...

Ecclesiastes 10:19

The Menu

Hamotzi made by _____

_____

Kiddush made by _____

_____

Hors d'oeuvres _____

_____

Appetizers _____

_____

Main Course _____

_____

Dessert _____

_____

Special toasts _____

_____

Other _____

MEMORIES OF THE PARTY

The chief highlight

_____

_____

The funniest moment

_____

_____

The most embarrassing moment

_____

_____

Additional memories

_____

_____

_____

_____

_____

MY BAR MITZVAH PARTY

The Lord of hosts [will] make unto
all peoples a feast...

Isaiah 25:6

Guest List

_____

_____

_____

_____

_____

_____

_____

_____

_____

_____

_____

_____

_____

_____

RIMMONIM (Torah Finials)—Frankfurt am Main, early 18th century

Guest List

_____

_____

_____

_____

_____

_____

_____

_____

_____

_____

_____

_____

_____

_____

_____

_____

_____

_____

_____

GUEST LIST

_____

_____

_____

_____

_____

_____

_____

_____

_____

_____

_____

_____

_____

_____

_____

_____

_____

GUEST LIST

_____

_____

_____

_____

_____

_____

_____

_____

_____

_____

_____

_____

_____

_____

_____

_____

TORAH CURTAIN (center section)—Galizia, 1795

GUEST LIST

_____

_____

_____

_____

_____

_____

_____

_____

_____

_____

_____

_____

_____

_____

_____

_____

_____

GUEST LIST

_____

_____

_____

_____

_____

_____

_____

_____

_____

_____

_____

_____

_____

_____

FROM	GIFT	THANK-YOU NOTE SENT

TALLIT, TALLIT BAG, AND TEFILLIN BAG—China, 1904

GIFTS

FROM	GIFT	THANK-YOU NOTE SENT
_____	_____	_____
_____	_____	_____
_____	_____	_____
_____	_____	_____
_____	_____	_____
_____	_____	_____
_____	_____	_____
_____	_____	_____
_____	_____	_____
_____	_____	_____
_____	_____	_____
_____	_____	_____
_____	_____	_____
_____	_____	_____
_____	_____	_____

GIFTS

FROM	GIFT	THANK-YOU NOTE SENT

FROM	GIFT	THANK-YOU NOTE SENT

READER'S DESK—Persia, c. 1900

It is good for a man that he bear
the yoke in his youth.

LAMENTATIONS 3:27

Thoughts I have had during my first thirteen years

_____

_____

_____

_____

My proudest and best moments

_____

_____

_____

My worst moment

_____

_____

_____

The desire accomplished is
sweet to the soul.

PROVERBS 13:19

Thoughts on what I would like to accomplish during my next thirteen years

My ambitions

_____

_____

Future professions _____

_____

The college of my choice _____

_____

How I can improve myself

_____

_____

_____

We only want that which is given naturally to all peoples, to be masters of our own fate, only of our fate, not of others, and in cooperation and friendship with others.

Golda Meir

President of the United States

_____

Vice President

_____

Prime Minister of Israel

_____

Headlines and special news events

_____

_____

_____

_____

_____

_____

MOSES LIFTING THE TABLETS OF THE LAW—Rembrandt van Rijn

MARK THE MAN OF INTEGRITY, AND BEHOLD
THE UPRIGHT: FOR THERE IS A FUTURE FOR THE
MAN OF PEACE.   PSALM 37:37

What My Faith Means To Me

_____

_____

_____

_____

_____

_____

_____

_____

_____

_____

_____

_____

_____

If I forget thee, O Jerusalem...

Psalm 137:5

What Israel Means To Me

_____

_____

_____

_____

_____

_____

_____

_____

_____

_____

_____

_____

_____

_____

Clothes _____

_____

Accessories _____

_____

Music _____

_____

Videos _____

_____

Electronics _____

_____

Sports _____

_____

Cars _____

_____

Sayings and phrases _____

_____

Other _____

_____

_____

BAR MITZVAH COAT—Bucharan, 19th century

my likes

My favorite movies _____

_____

My favorite TV shows _____

_____

My favorite stars _____

_____

My favorite music groups _____

_____

My favorite songs _____

_____

My favorite teams _____

_____

My favorite foods _____

_____

My favorite clothes _____

_____

My favorite possessions _____

_____

my dislikes

Music _____

_____

Singers and/or groups _____

_____

TV Shows _____

_____

Stars _____

_____

Sports _____

_____

School subjects _____

_____

Clothes _____

_____

Food _____

_____

Other things _____

_____

A friend loveth at all times...

PROVERBS 17:17

STUDYING THE TALMUD—Isidor Kaufman

TORAH CASE—Kaifeng, China, 17th century

And thou shalt love the Lord thy God with all thy heart, and with all thy soul, and with all thy might.

And these words which I command thee this day, shall be upon thy heart;

and thou shalt teach them diligently unto thy children...

Deuteronomy 6:5-7

I shall always remember this day, and will keep the memory of it dear to my heart. I shall recall all my impressions, and shall recount them to my children and grandchildren. It was indeed a special day when I became a man and could take my place within the community.